original art by
sam Harshbarger

ROBOT RHYMES

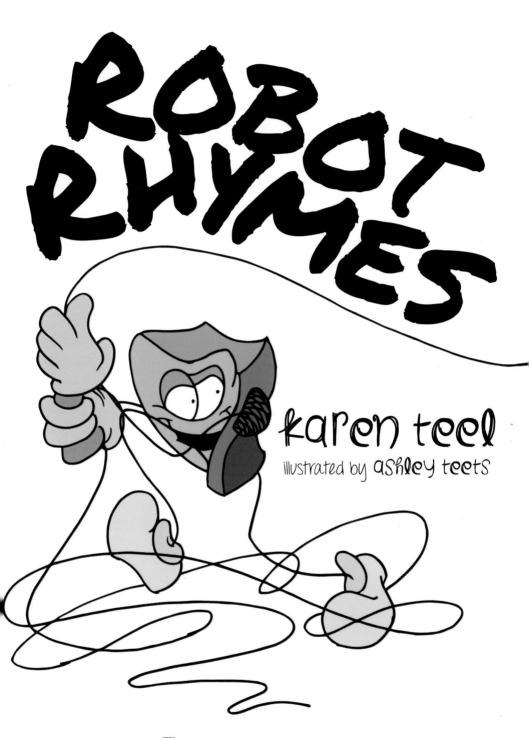

karen teel

illustrated by ashley teets

Headline Kids
an imprint of **Headline Books, Inc.**

Terra Alta, WV

by Karen Teel

illustrated by Ashley Teets

To order additional copies of this book or for book publishing information, or to contact the author:

Headline Kids
P. O. Box 52
Terra Alta, WV 26764
www.headlinekids.com

Tel: 800-570-5951
Email: mybook@headlinebooks.com
www.headlinebooks.com

Headline Kids is an imprint of Headline Books

ISBN-13: 978-0-938467-79-3

Library of Congress Control Number: 2013946296

PRINTED IN THE UNITED STATES OF AMERICA

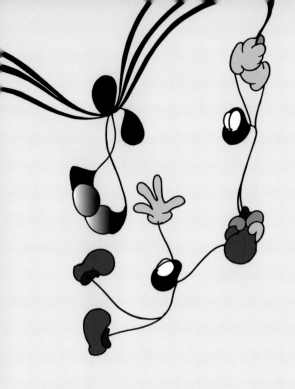

Dedicated to
Sam Harshbarger
Always in our hearts

It's a
beautiful day
out on robot
ranch

Little Snuggie's
steady kicking
out the robot
jams

Looking for
some answers-
just how, not why
Searching for direction

in the **robot**
rhymes

Listening to some truths that the **funkbots** know coming to him . . . ready? On time and on **tempo**

9

They tell him
break loose
from the
fool's
parade
You gotta mind?
step outta line.
Choose to
create.

11

Don't be gawking
at the
solar
system
rolling past
Oscillating in between
the moon
and solid
earth

See
the live show
with a
great
surprise
Get wide on the melody
and skate
the
skies.

15

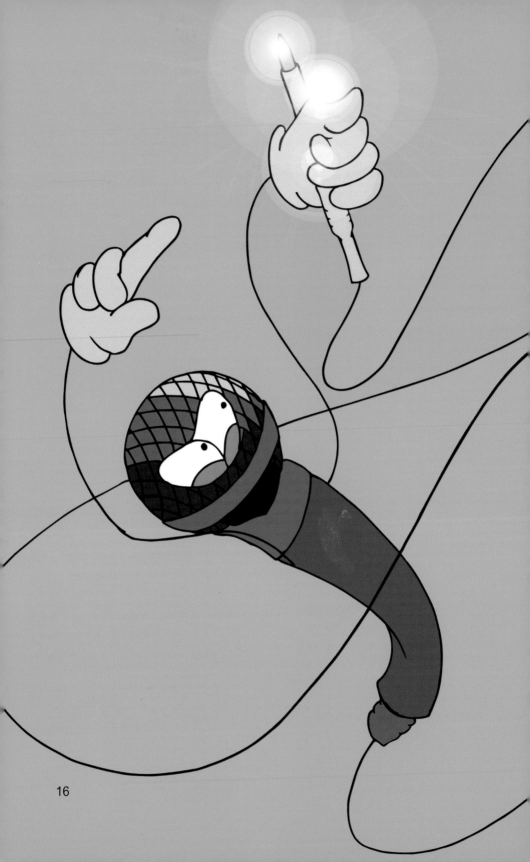

16

It only takes a
spark.
Bust a new style, snuggie.
Awesome is as
awesome
does
so get . . .
get busy!

Take some
chances
Take your
time
Listen where
the Robots are
dancing wide
Every little circuit
will be working well
And you can see your
soul
in its perfect shell

Keep tugging on
your own bootstraps
that's the word
But stay tied to your
kinfolk with a holy
bungee cord

(A biscuit smeared with preserves
reminds me of home in the hills,
with my fam behind me)

Get it straight,
   snuggie
There's
no better way
to **say** it
   It's inevitable, snuggie
   There's a
   better way to **play** it

There's
no good way
   to **could**
If you never, ever
   should
But there's no
   bad way to do it
   If you stay true to it

Keep liking
diamonds, snuggie
Keep liking quartz
Don't take no one for granted
Don't harbor hate nor hurt
Don't take the time
Lie prone in the grass
And gaze at other
planets.

psst...

Don't be limp-wristed
With a twisted aim
No coulda done this
No shoulda done that
It's that super-duper
jupiter jazz
Boom to the bap when you
do dat daa!

Life seems sorta
like a tease, Snuggie
It's brief
A piece off
a universal fabric

Now we've let you hear it right
Right here in the spirit life
Yeah, where the feeling's nice
Snuggie, make a
good life

He's had a
beautiful day out on
robot ranch
snuggie getting answers from
his **funkbot** friends
He's learned a lot
He won't fret the end
It's always a beginning somewhere
somewhen

GLOSSARY

funk – a style of music based on blues and soul

hip hop music – rhythmic music often including rhyming, chanted words and called rap music

jam – two or more musicians making music together

lyrics – the words of a song

melody – the arrangement of musical sounds in a song

oscillate – to vibrate or move to and fro

rhyme – verse in which the final sounds of lines agree

rhythm – the pattern of regular beats in music

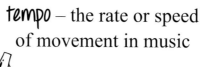

tempo – the rate or speed of movement in music